GEO ✓

EXTREME sports

rock climbing

BARRON'S

contents

Chris Craggs

Rock climbing began as a sport over 100 years ago. It has now spread to many countries of the world.

The idea is to climb rocks using only your hands and feet. The equipment, such as ropes, is for your safety — not to help you climb.

Rock climbing is great exercise for your body and your mind. It is a very exciting sport. Once you have learned the basics, you can go on to do harder and more thrilling climbs. It is a sport that will take you to amazing places that only rock climbers can reach.

Glenn Robbins

types of

rock climbing

There are six types of rock climbing. They are described in detail later in the book. All rock climbers climb on steep rugged rock or cliffs, which are found on mountains, sea cliffs, and abandoned quarries.

Trad climbing

(see pages 10–11)
Climbing with someone else using safety equipment that is fixed to the rock but can be taken out again. This equipment is called protection.

Sport climbing

(see pages 12-13)
Climbing with someone else using protection that is fixed to the rock and cannot be taken out again.

Soloing

(see pages 30–31)
Climbing alone using no safety equipment.

Bouldering

(see pages 24–25)
Climbing without protection on small cliffs.

Indoor climbing

(see pages 26–27)
Climbing on man-made indoor cliffs, called climbing walls. This is a good way to get started.

Competition climbing

(see pages 28–29)
Competitions include climbing with protection, and bouldering. The competitions take place on climbing walls.

equipment

Clothing
This is either tight-fitting and stretchy, or loose and baggy so that you can move easily. Most people wear sweat pants, lycra tights or leggings, and T-shirts. You can wear a fleece top if it's cold.

Harness
This is made from strong nylon tape. It is worn like a belt around the waist and also goes around the thighs. Its job is to attach the rope to the climber. It is also used to carry the protection.

Rock boots
These are light and tight-fitting. They have rubber soles to help you grip.

Belay plate

This is made of metal. It is attached to the harness with a krab — a metal clip. It is used to control the rope and help to hold a falling climber.

Ropes

These are made of nylon. They are light but very strong. Different sizes of rope are used for different types of climb.

Chalk bag

Powdered chalk is used to keep a climber's hands dry. It is carried in a bag tied around the waist.

Helmet

A helmet should always be worn by beginners to protect the head. Some expert climbers choose not to wear one.

the basics

Most rock climbing is done in pairs. The climbers are tied to either end of the rope.

The leader

The person who climbs first is called the leader. The leader is in the more dangerous position and must take care to protect himself in case of a fall. The leader climbs up the rock trailing a rope that is held by the other climber. The other climber is called the second. Controlling the rope for a partner is called belaying.

The rope is clipped into protection points using krabs. This means that if the leader makes a mistake, the rope will stop his fall before he hits the ground.

A krab

Glenn
Robbins

8

Belay
When the leader finishes the climb he attaches himself to the rock using more protection. The attachment is called a belay.

The second
The second then climbs the rock. The rope is held from above by the leader. As the second climbs, he removes the protection.

trad climbing

In this style of climbing, metal nuts are used as protection. The nuts are threaded on to rope or wire loops. They are jammed into cracks in the rock and linked to the rope by krabs. These are placed by the leader and removed by the second.

sport

climbing

In this style, metal bolts are used as protection. They are fixed to the rock in drilled holes and cannot be taken out again. The rope is attached to the bolts by krabs.

Glenn Robbins

Glenn Robbins

Sometimes at the top of the climb there is a fixed belay. The leader can thread the rope through this and be lowered back to the ground. He collects the krabs on the way down. This means that sometimes the second does not need to do the climb. Most climbing on climbing walls is done like this.

If there is no fixed belay at the top then the second must do the climb to get the krabs.

where to climb

Climbers' guidebooks tell you where the cliffs and the climbs are. The climbs — also known as routes — are described in these books.

There can be many routes on a cliff. Each one is given a name and a grade.

14

The first person to climb a new route up a cliff is the one who can name it.

Chris Craggs

The grade tells you how easy or difficult the climb is. This is important because trying to do a climb that is too difficult for you can be dangerous.

Chris Craggs

the rock

Types of cliff

There are three types of cliff — slabs, overhangs, and walls.

⬭ **Slab**
A cliff that leans back at an angle.

⬭ **Overhang**
A cliff that leans forward.

⬭ **Wall**
A cliff that goes straight up.

Holds

Climbers use parts of the rock called holds. These are lumps, dents, or cracks in the cliff that the climber can use to grip the rock. There are hand holds and foot holds and there are lots of different sizes (see the next page). Bigger holds usually mean that the climb is easier, but this also depends on the angle of the cliff.

Chris Craggs

Cracks

Cracks in the rock often give very good hand and foot holds. They can be so narrow that only fingers will fit in. They can also be so big that the whole climber can fit in. Sometimes you climb a crack the whole way up to the top of a cliff.

holds

There are different types of hold. They all have different names.

Hand jam
Fixing your hand into a crack in the rock. You can also do a **finger jam** or a **foot jam**.

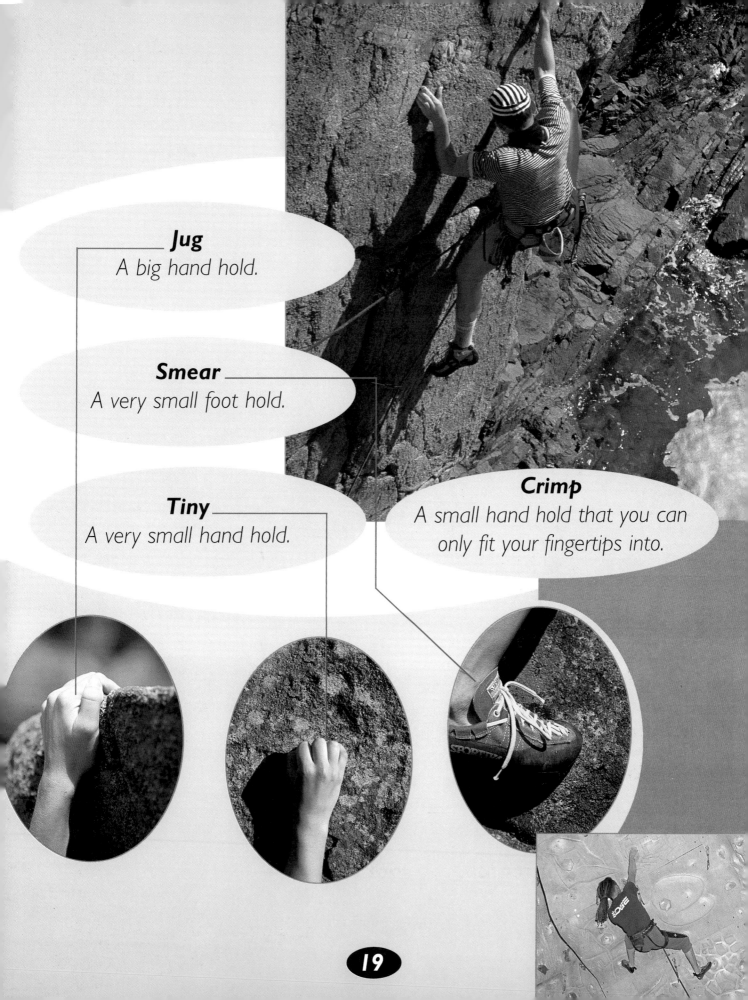

Jug
A big hand hold.

Smear
A very small foot hold.

Tiny
A very small hand hold.

Crimp
A small hand hold that you can only fit your fingertips into.

moves

You can climb rock using the different moves that are described here.

Laybacking

You can do this when there is a crack in the middle of a corner. You do it by pulling with your arms, and pushing against the rock with your feet. Your feet are often flat on the rock. Make small shuffling moves with your feet while reaching up with your hands.

Bridging

This is where you push against both sides of a corner or wide crack with your hands and feet stretched wide.

Chimneying

Use this move to climb a wide crack with your back against one wall. One foot is pushed against the rock in front of you, the other behind you. Make small shuffling moves upward by pushing down with your hands and feet and swapping them from one side of the crack to the other.

Heelhooking

Use this move to pull your body around an overhang. Put one heel up by your hands and use it as a lever to move your body.

moves plus

Traversing
Climbing sideways across a cliff.

Belaying
Controlling the rope while your partner is climbing.

Abseiling

Getting down a cliff by sliding down the rope in a controlled way.

Chris Craggs

Other words

*Protection equipment is called **gear**.*
*A climb without much protection is called a **serious route**.*

bouldering

Bouldering is climbing without safety equipment on small cliffs. The cliffs are small enough that you can fall or jump off them without hurting yourself.

If you have no one to climb with, try bouldering, which doesn't require a rope. It is very good for training. You can use it to learn new skills or try new moves. It can be fun to boulder with a group of friends.

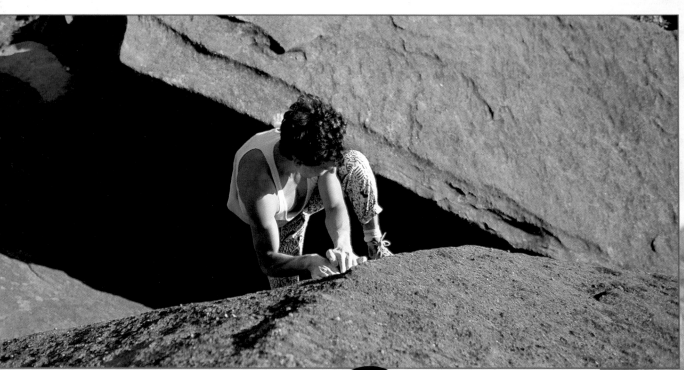

If the climb is too far off the ground to fall safely then it is no longer bouldering and becomes soloing (see pages 30–31).

climbing

walls

Most big towns and cities have climbing walls. You have to pay to use them and you may have to become a member of a club. Good climbing walls have many different slabs, walls, and overhangs. They have lots of different grades of climbing. Some clubs will give you lessons and let you rent equipment. Many have special children's climbing clubs. There is often a bouldering section.

Walls are great for —

○ learning the basics

○ training to get better

○ climbing when the weather is bad outdoors.

competitions

Competitions are held on climbing walls. There are junior and senior levels of competition. They can be held to find the best boulderer or the best leader.

Climbing walls are used for regional or national competitions. International competitions are held on specially built walls in sports arenas.

soloing

Soloing is the most exciting and the most dangerous style of climbing.

You climb trad or sport routes without a rope or protection. Any mistake you make will mean that you could be seriously hurt or killed in a fall.

Soloing should only be done by expert climbers who know the risks. But if you're good enough, and can stay cool, soloing can give you the best feeling of all.

Safety

Rock climbing is great fun and good exercise but it can be very dangerous. You need to be taught proper safety methods by an experienced climber or qualified instructor.

extra stuff

Disclaimer

In the preparation of this book all due care has been exercised with regard to the activities depicted. The Publishers regret that they can accept no liability for any loss or injury sustained.

Text and photos: Ian Smith (except where indicated)
Series editor: Matthew Parselle
Designer: Andy Stagg

First edition for the United States and Canada published exclusively by Barron's Educational Series, Inc., 1999.

First published in the United Kingdom 1998 by Franklin Watts, London
Copyright 1998 Franklin Watts

Address all inquiries to:
Barron's Educational Series, Inc.
250 Wireless Boulevard
Hauppauge, NY 11788
http://www.barronseduc.com

Library of Congress Catalog Card No. 98-73622

ISBN 0-7641-0801-8

Printed in Great Britain
9 8 7 6 5 4 3 2 1

Useful Contacts

American Mountain Guides Association
Tel: (303) 271-0984
Association of Canadian Mountain Guides
Tel: (403) 678-2885

Index

Chris Craggs